OCEAN SUITE

poems by

Clifford Bernier

Finishing Line Press
Georgetown, Kentucky

OCEAN SUITE

ACKNOWLEDGMENTS

With gratitude to the editors of the venues where these poems first appeared,
some in slightly different form:

Bourgeon, poetry posted by Gregory Luce: "Imagining"; "Awakening";
"Knowing"; "Brackish Marsh"; "Chromatic"; "Meaning".

Portraits of Life, An Ekphrastic Anthology: "Leading the Way" written to
painting by April M. Rimpo; "Turning the Page" written to painting by
Elaine Weiner-Reed.

EC Poetry and Prose "Country Life" Ekphrastic Exhibition: "Brook" written
to painting by April M. Rimpo.

David Froman, Choral Composer: "Singing"; "Beauty"; "Singing Too";
"Spoken", set to SAATBB A Cappella music.

Publisher: Leah Huete de Maines
Editor: Christen Kincaid
Cover Art: Clifford Bernier
Author Photo: Clifford Bernier
Cover Design: Elizabeth Maines McCleavy

Order online: www.finishinglinepress.com
also available on amazon.com

Author inquiries and mail orders:
Finishing Line Press
PO Box 1626
Georgetown, Kentucky 40324
USA

Contents

For Kyoko

From the beginning.

Sea's Edge

I stand at the sea's edge hoping the voice of the waves will bring meaning.

But the voice of the waves does not bring meaning.

At least hoping it brings words, which I hope will have hidden meanings.

But the hidden meanings of the words come without voice.

And not from the sea's edge, or hope, raucous with waves.

Deep Dive

Explore the space
between words.
Is a word hidden within—
a sinkhole, a tunnel,
a portal to a meaning
you can't know—
the flip side
of a word?
In this poem—
take a deep dive.
See the creatures
swimming there
in darkness, willingly,
each making its own
inscrutable light.

Sea Sound

The sea sounds peace
beyond my time.
As time moves the sound
of peace. Testament the tide,
shells, broken glass—
Is peace as silent as the sun -
As raucous as the moon -
the swaying, singing moon,
beyond the sea sound.

Singing

Singing like the sea grass to the heron in the marsh.

Singing like the egret to the swallow in the pine.

Singing like the plover to the otter in the reeds.

Singing like the guitars of Spanish moss.

Singing like the ibis to the strumming of the flounder.

Singing like the kingfish to the drumming of the swan.

Singing like the osprey to the chuckle of the oyster.

Singing like the loony, snagging sun.

Meaning

The meaning of the sun is the shape of the trees.

The meaning of the moon is the color of the night.

The meaning of the sea is the path on the shore.

The meaning of the land is the forest where I walk.

Brook

As the sea sounds peace
in the rough and tumble
though the voice of its waves
does not bring meaning—
unless peace is meaning,
a sound beyond time
or an ancient silence,
beyond even the brook's voice
and its song of field and forest,
spray and stone,
brave words knowing the way
back to the river, back to the sea.

Pacific Coast

If beauty is peace
and peace is meaning,
then beauty is meaning
and the folding waves
on this freckled beach
is meaning. Ask the gull
balancing the wind.
The driftwood on the bank.
Sea grass like mustard
on the dunes, and the
relentless mist. They know.

Sound

Sound implies no sound
but what the waves imply
is not absence. Compassing
like the sun or the rotating
stars, circling like night
or the rounding moon.
The early moon. Why
should peace be different—
in the fullness of silence
the same sun is perhaps setting
into the sea, beyond the sea.

Beauty

Beauty like the clatter of disaffected gulls.

Beauty like the glitter of freckled sand.

Beauty like the slender leaning huddled firs.

Beauty like the nourishing rain.

Beauty like the sea grass tossing in the breeze.

Beauty like the driftwood tumbling to the shore.

Beauty like the calls of colluding cormorants.

Beauty like the stepping, stumbling surf.

Syllables

What are the syllables of the sea—
the currents and tides of meaning—
the dune grass, the sparrow, the gull,
the shore pine, the pea, the yarrow—
the folding waves like sibilants,
the restless breeze like breath—
voicing a grammar beyond my time,
elements of words without etymology—
beyond the whimbrel, the dunlin, the grebe—
diction without dictionary—
spoken in being on this wind-speckled beach,
knowing all there is to know.

Waves

The layered, frothy waves,
blown from the rim of the world.
The slipping sea flat as a mirror.
See that the sky is as gray
as the swells, a perfect reflection,
as the sound of the waves
is of the silence beyond, the
silence within, the silence everywhere.

Beyond

That the beyond is here
is self-evident. As is now.
And the speaking sea.
As the silence that makes
the sea's song its sound.
The hopeful surf, the lark,
the tern— mirrored in the
raucous fullness of peace.
Obvious too the bleached clams,
the crab claws, the barnacles—
by the flotsam of the past.
Uncluttered but perhaps
shimmering as the heron leaping
in the reflective light
to the sliding moon and
the roaring, strutting sea.

Singing Too

Singing like the mallard to the swinging of the moon.

Singing like the sea foam to the dancing of the dune grass.

Singing like the shore pine to the croaking of the treefrog.

Singing like the spinning, sparkling wind.

Singing like the cockle to the cackle of the clam.

Singing like the swallow to the swishing of the brant.

Singing like the condor to the complaining coot.

Singing like the swirling, swelling sea.

Chromatic Run

Chromatic the light on the breathing lake,
on the leaning bark, on the biting bird.

Chromatic the light on the leaning lake,
on the breathing bark, on the bouncing bird.

Chromatic the light on the laughing lake,
on the biting bark, on the barking bird.

Chromatic the light on the barking lake,
on the bouncing bark, on the laughing bird.

Brackish Marsh

In the brackish marsh
I am a dog in a duck's eye,
more jester than jockey,
more joker than juror.
When beavers dance
I am a goat in a goose's dream,
at water's edge
I am a freak in a frog's leap,
a madman in a muskrat's march,
a monster in a mallard's mind.
More clumsy than careful,
more cartoon than contender.

Marsh Words

When words have run dry
like the marsh in mid-winter
I cannot use osprey or egret—
heron and stork are depleted
and duck is out of stock.
What words remain are elusive—
and reclusive— since birds are
birds and words are words.

Imagining

Imagine light unpeeling
like apple skin,
or a cloud of crows
circling,
from a woodland pond
reflecting
trees above
regarding me with wonder,
imagining me.

Awakening

See morning unpeel
like an orange,
loop the merry-
go-round sun and
once
again
churn me
to butter,
spread me thick
on baguette
like marmalade.
See light plink
a backyard pond
in horizons,
swing
and swoop me
like fin-flash
to the moon.
And see my cup
drip with jelly,
toys
toast and figs
sprung
by awakening.

Knowing

Watch days peel off
like grapes,
green as gum
sweet as wine
swift in twilight
twisting
like wings
tableau of stem
branch
and skin
plucking bunches,
knowing me.

Leading the Way

The leader knows
language only goes so far—
that waves say more
than words will
and gulls gathering at noon
sort the polemics of the world.

Leading the way
through the crowd of ash
to the slightest syllable
crashing like surf—
there will always be another.

Since the end is the beginning
as T.S. said
and to paraphrase W.S.
Not knowing is the mother of wonder.

Turning the Page

As the juxtaposition of words
reveals hidden meanings,
and as summer renders autumn
with new meaning—
like rolling surf
let's flip the page.

The maple are iridescent
red within green,
their words lead to waves repeating
like recitation—
leaves of this book
that keep turning.

And the wind tumbling
toward winter
is the last word of the last poem
that explains everything—
and nothing, juxtaposed with spring.

Without Sound

What lives without sound—
is meaning only in sound?
The cherry blossoming life,
the maple signaling spring,
the azalea beginning to bud—
birds chirp and squirrels chat
but the evergreen is full,
the sky is clear as the lake
and the earth is still.
Sunlight illumines the leaves.

Sound Without Words

Sound without words
and words without sound—
my inner voice that makes
meaning from silence—
like ripples on the lake,
branches drifting in the sun
and drywood on the bank—
How different the bird calls,
the diving duck, needles
sifting the breeze, wood
pecker pecking— from
shadows on the far shore,
the white throats of geese,
the flapping mallard,
musings of my meandering mind—

River

Sound is the
river and the
meaning
of the wind
in this refuge
near the James.
As the logic that
swirls to the sea.
Of contradictions
and paradoxes
dropped into
difference.
Of the restless
popping
of time
and thought
that separates
from it in
the moment
and merging
of sound
and meaning.

Spoken

Spoken in being like the silver bay.

Spoken in being like the ferry crossing.

Spoken in being like the sheltering cedars.

Spoken in being like the frosty wake.

Spoken in being like the guiding stars.

Spoken in being like the gliding moon.

Spoken in being like the shorebird call.

Spoken in being like the sea.

Time and Place

Beyond time and place—
after the final wave
but current with it—
a space without condors
but filled with beauty.
The killdeer and the scaup.
The pintail and the
bufflehead. Mirrored
in the fullness of
silence. Peaceful
like the slide of the sea.
The is and the is and the is.
The now and the now.
Spoken like meaning.

Clifford Bernier's *The Silent Art* won the Gival Press Poetry Award. He is also the author of *Dark Berries* and *Earth Suite*, each selected by the *Montserrat Review* as a Best Chapbook. He appears in *The Write Blend* poetry circle collection among other print and online journals and anthologies. In addition, Mr. Bernier appears on harmonica in the Portuguese *Accumulated Dust* world music series and is featured on the EP *Post-Columbian America*. He has been featured in readings in Los Angeles, Seattle, Chicago, Buffalo, Detroit, Philadelphia, Baltimore, and the Washington, DC area, including the Library of Congress, the Arts Club of Washington, George Washington University (where he is a member of the Washington Writer's Collection) and the Bethesda Writer's Center. He has been a reader for the Washington Prize and a judge for the National Endowment for the Arts' Poetry Out Loud recitation contest. From 2003-2008 he hosted the *Poesis* reading series in Arlington, Virginia and performed with the Jazzpoetry band at venues in and around Washington, DC. He has been nominated for two Pushcart Prizes and a Best of the Net Award. He lives with his family in Alexandria, Virginia.

www.ingramcontent.com/pod-product-compliance
Lightning Source LLC
Chambersburg PA
CBHW022059080426
42734CB00009B/1418